The Nature Kid's Guide to

BEETLES

Level 2

DAVID ANDERSON

For information address LP Media Inc. Publishing,
30012 Variolite St NW, Princeton MN 55371
www.lpmedia.org

Publication Data

Beetles
The Nature Kid's Guide to Beetles — First edition.

Summary: "Learn all about Beetles, the Nature Kid Way"
— Provided by publisher.

ISBN: 979-8-89818-188-8

[1. Beetles – Non-Fiction] I. Title.

Title: The Nature Kid's Guide to Beetles

CONTENTS

BEETLE BONANZA

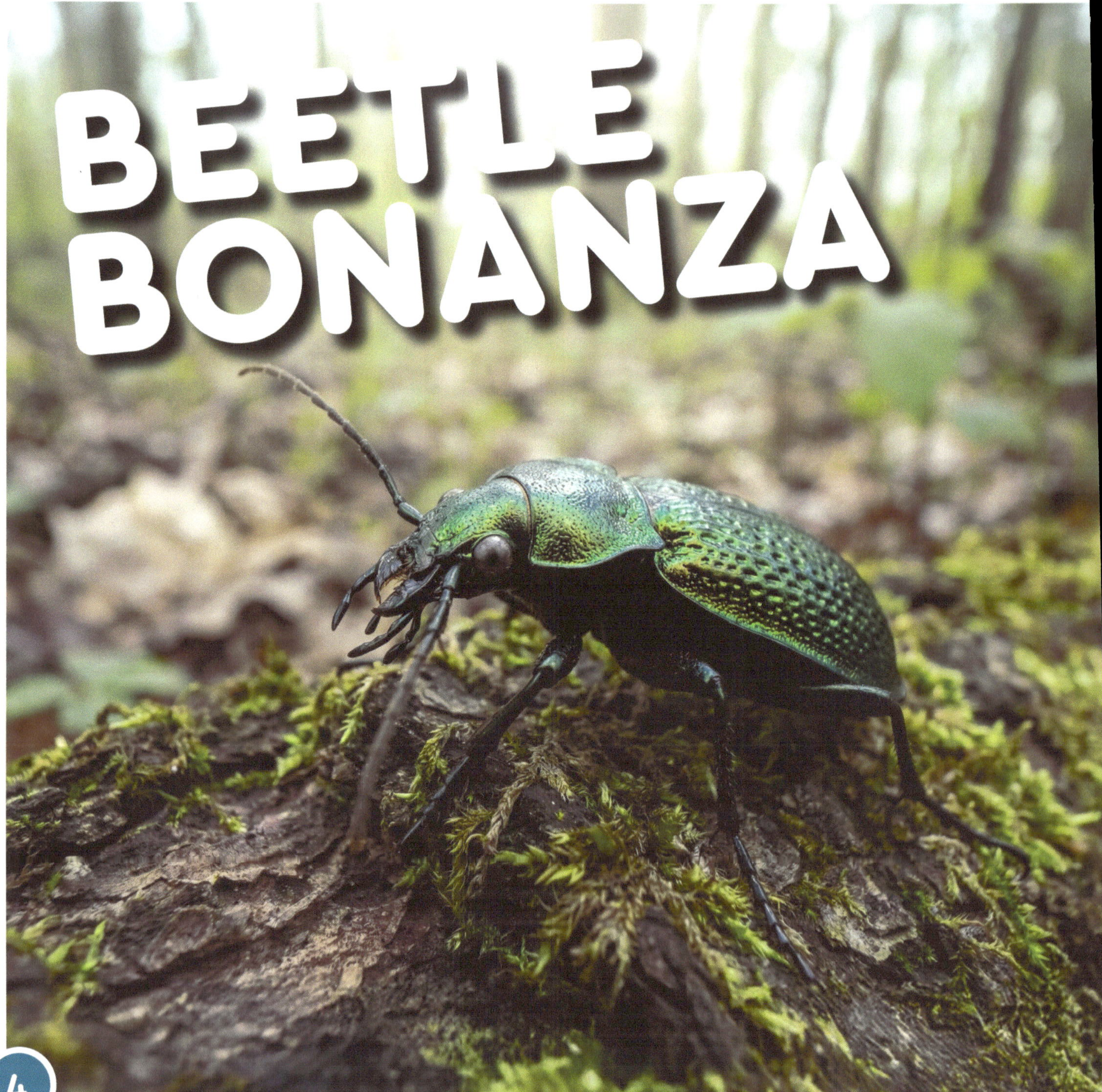

Buzz! A shiny ground beetle crawls on a log in the forest.

Beetles live all over the world. You can find them in forests, deserts, ponds, and even your backyard. They come in many shapes and sizes.

There are more kinds of beetles than any other insect. Scientists have found over 400,000 types so far. That means one out of every four animal species on Earth is a beetle!

Some beetles are tiny as a grain of sand. Others are as big as your hand. No matter the size, every beetle is amazing in its own way.

If you counted one beetle species every second, it would take you five days straight to count them all!

WINGS OF ARMOR

A beetle's hard wing covers meet in a perfectly straight line down its back – like a tiny zipper!

Click! A Ladybug opens its shell to stretch its wings.

Beetles come in all shapes, sizes, and colors. But no matter how different they look, every beetle is built the same way.

All beetles have six legs and two feelers called antennae on their head. The feelers help them smell food and find their way around. They also have strong jaws for biting and chewing.

Every beetle has two pairs of wings. The top pair is called the **elytra**. It is hard and tough, like a suit of armor. When a beetle wants to fly, it lifts that armor up and out of the way. Then the soft wings underneath start to flap, and off it goes!

SUPER BEETLES

Zing! A stag beetle dodges a bird and flies off safely.

Beetles are full of surprises. Some glow in the dark. Others spray boiling hot gas at enemies. A few can even swim underwater like tiny submarines!

Strong horns help some beetles push and fight. Hard shells protect others from hungry birds. Bright colors warn predators to stay far away.

Some beetles escape danger with super-fast legs. Others hide by blending in with bark or leaves. No matter the trick, every beetle has its own way to survive.

LOVELY LADYBUG

Crunch! A ladybug chomps down on a tiny green aphid.

You have probably seen a ladybug before. These tiny red and orange beetles with black spots show up in gardens, fields, and parks all over the world. But there is a lot more to them than their pretty shells!

Ladybugs are hungry little hunters. They love to eat **aphids**, tiny bugs that harm plants by sucking their juice. One ladybug can gobble up 50 aphids in a single day!

When scared, ladybugs ooze yellow goo from their legs. Birds and frogs think it tastes so gross they leave ladybugs alone. Not bad for such a little beetle!

LIVING LANTERNS

In some forests, thousands of fireflies sync up and flash together at the exact same moment!

12

Flash! A tiny light blinks on and off in the dark grass.

Fireflies are not flies at all. They are beetles! On warm summer nights, fireflies light up fields and yards like living stars. Each kind of firefly has its own special flash pattern.

The light comes from a special part on their belly. Two chemicals inside mix together and create a glow with no heat at all. It is like having a tiny flashlight built right into your body! Fireflies flash to find a mate in the darkness.

Baby fireflies can glow too. They start as eggs and glow even before they hatch. People call these glowing babies "glowworms".

STAR GAZERS

Plop! A dung beetle rolls a ball of poop across the ground.

Dung beetles eat and use animal poop. It sounds gross, but this job is very important! Dung beetles clean up the land and help the soil.

Some dung beetles roll poop into big round balls. They push each ball with their back legs, walking backward. Then they bury it underground to feed their babies.

At night, dung beetles look up at the stars. They use the Milky Way to roll in a straight line. No other insect navigates by starlight!

One dung beetle can bury poop 250 times its own weight in a single night!

STAG BATTLES

Clash! Two stag beetles lock their giant jaws together.

Stag beetles get their name from their huge jaws. The jaws look like the antlers on a deer. Male stag beetles use them to wrestle other males in fierce battles.

Two males grab each other and push hard. Each one tries to flip the other off a branch. The winner gets to stay near the female, while the loser tumbles away.

Stag beetles live in forests with old trees. Their babies grow inside rotting logs for years. Without dead wood, these amazing beetles cannot survive.

HERCULES CHAMPION
FUN FACT!
The Hercules beetle can lift 850 times its own weight. That's like you picking up ten elephants!
18

Nibble! A Hercules beetle has found his lunch. It's rotting fruit!

Hercules beetles are some of the longest beetles on Earth. Males have a giant horn on their head and one on their back. The two horns work together like pincers to grab and squeeze.

These beetles live in rain forests in Central and South America. They munch on rotting fruit on the forest floor. Their big bodies can grow up to 7 inches long—as long as your hand!

Males use their horns to fight over mates. They grab rivals and lift them into the air. The strongest beetle wins and gets to stay.

HORN POWER

DID YOU KNOW?

In Japan, kids keep rhinoceros beetles as pets and hold beetle wrestling matches!

Thud! A rhinoceros beetle crawls over a fallen tree trunk.

Rhinoceros beetles have a big horn on their head. It looks just like a rhino's horn. Only the males grow this impressive weapon.

These beetles are incredibly strong for their size. They can push through soil and bark with ease. They live in warm forests around the world, from Asia to the Americas.

At night, they come out to eat tree sap and fruit. Bright lights can confuse them, though. They fly toward the glow by mistake and bump into windows.

GOLIATH GIANTS

Wow! A Goliath beetle is almost the size of your hand!

Goliath beetles are one of the heaviest insects on Earth. They live in the tropical forests of Africa and can weigh about two ounces. For a beetle, that is enormous!

Males have a small Y-shaped horn for battling other males. Females have a flat head that helps them dig into soil to lay eggs.

Most of their lives are spent underground as big, chubby grubs eating rotting wood until they transform into adults.

Baby Goliath beetles are bigger than the adults! The grubs can grow almost 10 inches long.

SPEEDY BUGS

Zoom! A tiger beetle races across the hot sand like a blur.

Tiger beetles are the fastest running insects on Earth. They zoom across sand and dirt at 5 miles per hour to catch **prey**. Their long legs carry them at incredible speed.

But here is the wild part: these beetles run so fast they go temporarily blind! Their eyes cannot keep up with their legs. They have to stop, look around, spot their prey, and then sprint again.

If a tiger beetle were human-sized, it could run 480 miles per hour, way faster than a race car!

BOILING BLASTER

Splash! A bombardier beetle shoots boiling spray at a predator!

Bombardier beetles have an amazing defense trick. When danger is near, they shoot hot liquid from their rear end! The spray reaches 212 degrees. That is as hot as boiling water!

Inside the beetle, two chemicals mix together. When they meet, boom! The mix turns super hot and shoots out in a cloud of stinky spray.

This tiny beetle can aim its spray in any direction it wants. Ants, spiders, and frogs all learn to stay far away. Nobody wants to mess with this little blaster!

GLITTERING GEMS

28

Flutter! A jewel beetle shines like a tiny flying rainbow.

Jewel beetles glow with green, blue, gold, and red colors. Their shiny shells bounce light like tiny mirrors. These dazzling beetles live in warm forests and woodlands around the world.

The bright colors are not just for show. They help jewel beetles blend in with wet, shiny leaves. Birds can mistake them for harmless drops of water!

Female jewel beetles lay their eggs in tree bark. The babies live inside the wood as they grow, munching tunnels through the tree.

BUBBLE DIVERS

Splash! A diving beetle plunges below the pond's surface.

Diving beetles live in ponds, lakes, and slow streams. They have flat back legs shaped like paddles for swimming. These beetles are fierce hunters under water.

A diving beetle traps a bubble of air under its wings before it dives. This air bubble lets it breathe while swimming deep below. It is like carrying a tiny scuba tank everywhere!

Diving beetles eat tadpoles, small fish, and water bugs. They grab prey with their strong front legs and hold tight. Even animals bigger than them are not safe from these underwater hunters!

IRON ARMOR

DID YOU KNOW?
An ironclad beetle can survive being run over by a car. That's 39,000 times its own weight!

Peck! A bird bites down, but the ironclad beetle is just fine.

The ironclad beetle is one of the toughest bugs on Earth. Its shell is so hard that a bird cannot bite through it. This tough little tank lives in dry parts of North America.

This beetle cannot fly at all. Its wing covers are locked together like a welded shield. This makes the shell extra strong and almost impossible to break.

Scientists study this beetle's amazing armor. They want to know how the shell stays so tough. What they learn could help people build stronger airplanes and buildings!

FLAT FIDDLE

DID YOU KNOW?
A violin beetle is so flat it
could slide under a closed
door!

Swish! A paper-thin beetle slides under a layer of bark.

Violin beetles have a flat, wide body shaped like a violin. They live in rain forests in Southeast Asia. Their paper-thin shape helps them fit into the tiniest spaces.

These beetles hide between layers of wet bark on trees. They squeeze into cracks where other bugs cannot follow. This is where they find food and stay safe from predators.

When bothered, a violin beetle can squirt stinky goo. It tastes terrible and keeps enemies away. Being flat has never been so useful!

SUPER BEETLES

Munch! A Japanese beetle chews a dead leaf and feeds the soil below.

Beetles do big jobs for our planet. Many beetles break down dead plants and animals. This puts nutrients back in the soil so new plants can grow strong.

Some beetles spread **pollen** from flower to flower. This helps new plants grow and make seeds. Without beetles, many forests and gardens would struggle to survive.

Beetles are also food for birds, bats, frogs, and fish. They are a key part of the **food chain**. When beetles do well, the whole web of nature stays healthy and balanced.

PLANET CHAMPIONS

Ancient Egyptians believed scarab beetles were magical and wore them as lucky charms!

Snap! A six-spotted tiger beetle gets ready for a new day.

Next time you see a beetle, take a closer look before you say "ew!" That little creature might be wearing a suit of armor, glowing in the dark, or carrying a horn bigger than its head.

Beetles have been around for over 300 million years. They were here before the dinosaurs and are still going strong. With over 400,000 species, there are more kinds of beetles than almost any other animal on Earth!

From tiny ladybugs in your backyard to giant Goliaths in the African jungle, beetles are some of the most amazing creatures on the planet!

GLOSSARY

elytra
The hard wing covers that protect a beetle's soft flying wings

aphids
Tiny bugs that suck juice from plant stems

pollen
Fine powder inside flowers that helps make new plants

prey
An animal that is hunted and eaten by another animal

food chain
The order of who eats whom in nature